The
SEELBACH HILTON

❧

*A Centennial Salute
to Louisville's Grand Hotel*

Larry Johnson

BUTLER BOOKS
LOUISVILLE

ISBN 978-1-935497-49-3

Printed in Canada by Friesens Printers

For information, contact the publisher:

Butler Books
P.O. Box 7311, Louisville, KY 40257
502-897-9393
ckbutler@aol.com
www.butlerbooks.com

Dedication

I dedicate this book to my wife Betty, daughter Stephanie, son-in-law Kevin, and two very special little people, Garrett and Emma, my grandchildren.

Special dedication to Bill Butler (4/7/1949–7/8/2009)

Without his knowledge, insight and love of his family and the City of Louisville, this book would not have been possible.

Acknowledgments

This book pays tribute to all associates who have dedicated themselves to preserving the Seelbach's elegance, charm and dignity for 100 years.

Through their loyalty, the Seelbach remains the best hotel in Louisville and the Midwest, as it was in 1905.

To the special people in the last 30 years—Roger Davis, who had the dream of restoring the Seelbach, and all associates who have come and gone.

To those who have passed away while working for the hotel— John Young, a young bellman who came to work for the Seelbach when he was 82 years old; Max Allen, a third generation bartender; and Curtis Brown, a valet/bellman.

To the general managers, each doing it his own way—Thomas Payne (1982–1984); Mike Carnovale (1985–1995), who turned the hotel around and helped raise the occupancy; Dave Nichols (1995– 1998), who continued the success of the hotel; Larry Hollingsworth (1998–2004), one of the best businessmen with whom I have ever had the opportunity to work; Jon McFarland (2004–present), for keeping the Seelbach going during the ice storm, fire and flood renovations. Thanks to these gentlemen for making the hotel great.

To the one special lady who has stayed with the hotel for 28 years—Ethel Firch. To Brandt Ford, my "Seelbach boss" and friend, who gave me the guidance to do my job and the wisdom to do it right the first time. Also, Kelly P., for pushing me into writing about the Seelbach, and to my two assistant bell captains, Lyman Reynolds and Gary Gibson. Also, to James Smith for information he obtained from the Filson Club and Mrs. Jean Seelbach, Otto Seelbach, Jr.'s wife.

Very special thanks to Betty Johnson, the love of my life for 45 years, for doing all the typing and arranging the Seelbach stories contained in this book.

Special thanks to the University of Louisville and Louisville Free Public Libraries for all their help with research.

Also, special thanks to the two men, Louis and Otto Seelbach, who had a dream 115 years ago, and through drive and determination built Louisville's Grand Hotel, the Seelbach.

To our former and current mayors, Jerry Abramson and Greg Fischer, for helping to keep our city great.

The Seelbach—Above and Beyond

So gracious and splendid, if only the walls could talk,
So beautiful and old, with just a touch of new to enhance the view.
Like a majestic queen with all her elegant attire.
Her doors are always open to show off her heart and soul within.

So royal is the view the first time you see her lobby.
The paintings of history so brilliantly done
Reminds us of time gone by, but not forgotten.
Those lovely chandeliers hanging so delicately and strong.
Her beauty and grace, her charm and glow
Will always leave you in a spin.

—Larry Johnson
1986

Courtesy of the University of Louisville Photographic Archives
Caufield & Shook 85776

■ *The Seelbach Hotel,*
Fourth Street, 1927

This One Street Makes Louisville

"Stranger, would you solve the mysteries of our city?
Go then to 4th Avenue, for there beats the pulse.
You'll come away baffled, but pleased."

—*Courier-Journal*, August 3, 1919

■ *The Seelbach Hotel, Fourth Street, 2011*

■ *The Rathskeller*

A Brief Timeline of the Seelbach Hilton Hotel

1869 Louis Seelbach travels to Louisville from Bavaria and begins working in prominent Louisville hotels.

1874 Louis opens Seelbach's Restaurant and Café at Tenth and Main Streets.

1880 After much success, the restaurant moves to larger quarters at Sixth and Main.

1885 Louis, joined by his 22-year-old brother, Otto, form the Seelbach Hotel Company.

1886 The brothers open a 30-room hotel above the restaurant.

1888 Ten new rooms are added to the hotel.

1890 A 10-year renovation project begins, turning the Seelbach into a major, European-style hotel.

1900 The remodeled Seelbach reopens to immediate success. Women are admitted for the first time, with the all-male Union Club moving to the top floor.

1902 The Seelbach Realty Co. is formed to build the brothers' dream hotel from the ground up at the corner of Fourth and Walnut (now Muhammad Ali Blvd).

1905 The new Seelbach Hotel opens by throwing the biggest party in Louisville history. The hotel was so successful that the brothers began a 154-room addition in the fall, spending another $300,000.

1907 The new expansion is completed, featuring the now-famous Bavarian-style Rathskeller, decorated with rare Rookwood pottery.

1918 F. Scott Fitzgerald stays at the Seelbach, inspiring him to later use the hotel as the scene of Tom and Daisy Buchanan's wedding in his 1925 novel *The Great Gatsby*.

1923 Louisville author Cordia Greer Petrie publishes *Angeline at the Seelbach*. It lasts 30 editions and is made into a nationally-aired radio show.

1925 Louis Seelbach dies. His brother Otto and Louis' son, William, continue to run the hotel.

1926 The Seelbach is sold to Chicago investor Abraham M. Liebling for $2.5 million.

1929 Otto Seelbach retires in February, and the hotel is sold to Eppley Hotels, an Omaha firm.

1934 The Rathskeller reopens after Prohibition is repealed.

1937 The 1937 flood hits the city; the hotel escapes major damage with emergency generators and private wells.

1941 The hotel opens The Plantation Room nightclub in a space formerly leased to a drugstore.

1945 The hotel's basement, including the Rathskeller, is leased to the American Legion as a private club. The hotel begins major renovations.

1947 Democratic candidate for governor Earle Clements uses room 743 to plan his successful election campaign, inspiring others to do the same until 1971.

1948 Exterior remodeling adds a granite face to the first floor, eliminates one of two Fourth Street entrances, and adds one on Walnut Street.

1956 The Sheraton hotel chain purchases the Seelbach and begins a $1.1 million renovation, renaming the hotel The Sheraton.

1960 The Rathskeller reopens as a dinner theater.

1966 The Sheraton spends $500,000 in redecoration, renovation and painting to compete with suburban hotels.

1968 Gotham Hotels becomes the new owner of The Sheraton, and changes the name back to the Seelbach.

1975 The hotel closes, a victim of downtown deterioration from the flight of hotel guests to the suburbs.

1978 Actor Roger Davis and construction company owner Gil Whittenberg buy the hotel for $1 million and begin renovation and restoration to its original glory.

1981 Metropolitan Life Insurance obtains 50% of the Seelbach in return for a $15.5 million loan.

■ *The Oakroom*

1982 The Seelbach reopens in April, restored to its former grandeur. The reopening ceremonies include Louisville Mayor Harvey Sloane and Governor John Y. Brown, Jr.

1982–1990 The hotel is managed by National Hotels Corporation, a subsidiary of Radisson Hotels and Doubletree Hotels.

1983 The Seelbach is selected by the Preferred Hotels Association, one of only 40 hotels worldwide.

1990 The Seelbach is sold to Medallion Hotels of New York.

1995 The addition of the 8,678-square-foot Medallion Ballroom makes the hotel a top conference hotel in Louisville.

1996 The Oakroom undergoes renovations and reopens, aiming for a five-star level of quality.

1998 Meristar Hotels and Resorts purchases the Seelbach and begins a $10 million renovation of all guest rooms. The hotel begins proudly flying the Hilton flag and enjoying four-star, four-diamond status.

1999 The Oakroom receives AAA's Five Diamond designation.

2001 The Oakroom is entered into the Fine Dining Hall of Fame by *Nation's Restaurant News*.

2007 Investcorp International, Inc. purchases the hotel.

2009 Investcorp completely renovates the hotel—$14 million.

2017 A partnership between Rockbridge Capital from Columbus, Ohio, and Musselman Hotels Management, a Louisville-based company, purchases the hotel in December, 2017.

CHAPTER ONE
The Beginning, 1869

Louis Seelbach came to the United States in 1869. He eventually settled in Louisville, Kentucky and went to work for the original Galt House Hotel at the corner of Second and Main Streets. Mr. A.K. Cooper taught Louis everything he could about the hotel business, including the bar and restaurant business.

In 1874, Louis turned 22 and wanted to do something more with his life than work for the Galt House. Louis opened the Seelbach Bar & Grill that year. The bar was an instant success.

The bar was at the corner of Tenth and Main Street, in the middle of the business district of Louisville. The bar's visitors were businessmen from all the different types of shops, stores, and warehouses in the downtown at that time.

By 1879, the city was growing, businesses were thriving, and river and railroad traffic were bringing more people to Louisville. At this time there were about a dozen hotels in the city.

Otto Seelbach, who had been in banking in Frankenthal, Germany, soon came to Louisville to work with his brother. The two brothers moved their bar from Tenth and Main to the corner of Sixth and Main. The bar became the most popular bar in Louisville, with people coming from all over town to see the European Seelbach Bar & Grill. Feeding on that success, in 1890 the brothers decided they wanted to own and run a hotel. They closed the bar and started redoing the rooms on the top floors. When they were finished in 1891, they had 30 sleeping rooms and the best bar in town. The building the brothers turned into a hotel was the first European

■ *Louis Seelbach (left) and Otto Seelbach (right).*

■ *The Seelbach European Hotel, Sixth and Main Streets, 1892.*

Seelbach Hotel and the building still stands today, housing government offices and the Louisville Bar Association. In its honor there is a brick marker on the sidewalk in front of the door.

In 1902 the Seelbach brothers, with the help of some investors, formed the Seelbach Realty Company. There was a piece of property for sale at the corner of Fourth and Walnut (now Muhammad Ali) where a Mr. Ross had his small store. It was just a small neighborhood market, which was in Louisville's first residential area. The Realty company bought the property and started construction of what was to be the finest hotel in the city.

When construction started, the mayor of Louisville visited the site and told the brothers they were crazy for building their hotel so far away from the city center. The city then was only about three blocks north-to-south and twelve blocks east-to-west. Residential areas started at Jefferson Street. The mayor said, "No one will come to a hotel so far away." Luckily for the city and the business district of Louisville, no one listened to the mayor and other politicians who thought it would not be a success.

On April 30, 1905, Seelbach Realty Co. decided to have a stockholders' party to precede the Grand Opening the following night. The party would be a warmup for the staff. It was a grand event, but only a tease. Little did the staff know what the next night would have in store for them.

Grand Opening, May 1, 1905

The dream was about to become a reality, and the wait was worth the effort the brothers and Seelbach Realty had gone through. The night was a gala, with dinner parties in every room. The day started with about 25,000 people coming through the front doors into the lobby and pushing out the back doors.

The visitors seeing the hotel for the first time were amazed. The hotel was designed with the French Renaissance in mind. The exterior was made of stone and dark-pressed brick, ten stories tall, making it the first skyscraper in Louisville. The building and site cost $990,000, and the furnishings cost another $120,000.

The construction started in December, 1903 and was completed May 1, 1905, just in time for that year's Kentucky Derby.

Louis and Otto Seelbach greeted all sightseers from 10:00 a.m. until 3:00 p.m., when the doors were closed to make ready for the grand opening Gala at 6:00 p.m.

That night seven women fainted because of the jam of people and had to be carried to rooms to be revived, then sent out the back door where Louis Seelbach had a carriage take them home.

Traffic was at a standstill on Fourth and Walnut Streets, where people fought for hours to gain admittance. It took 15 policemen an hour to clear the hotel. Women predominated and many of the dresses were torn in the jam. Over 2000 people were turned away from the afternoon viewing.

The day was filled with excitement. To no one's surprise, this hotel that was built in the middle of a row housing area was a fantastic display of European charm and elegance. Pictures adorned the tops of the three main walls. These pictures were painted by Arthur Thomas and told a story of Kentucky history as seen through his eyes. Thomas painted the scenes on plaster so they would stay for all time.

The large painting on the left wall above the hall to the main elevators is "The First Peace Treaty", signed by the Indians. Seated in white buckskins is George Rogers Clark.

The painting above the front desk is the first Kentucky Legislative meeting. Daniel Boone sits to the right with his hand on his knee.

The large painting above The Old Seelbach Bar is called "The Crossings." It is a depiction of George Rogers Clark crossing the Wabash River.

■ *The hotel in May, 1905*

The skylight and small lamps were all the lighting in the lobby for the grand opening. There was a giant champagne fountain in the center. The sightseers could take a drink or just look at the beautiful lobby and all of its trim.

On May 1, people saw for the first time marble from Italy, Germany, and France, and wood from the West Indies and Europe. There were bronzes from France and linens from Ireland and the best of every material that could be had in this country.

Most of the furniture was solid mahogany, and some of it soon took medals at the St. Louis World Fair.

There were 1500 reservations for dinner in the dining room and café, with a seating capacity of only 300. Dinners were served at 6, 8 and 10 p.m. One hundred fifty guests slept in the hotel on opening night.

The staff for the grand opening consisted of 300 men, women and boys. The payroll was approximately $12,000 per month.

Mrs. Mary Durbeck, wife of Louis Seelbach, who looked after the comfort of the women visitors, said the crowd was the most wonderful sight she had ever seen.

The scene at 8:00 was brilliant. The main dining room, café and parlors were crowded with those who wished to drink to the success of the new hotel. On the top of the roof garden trellis was a fringe of electric lights that could be seen blocks away.

Louisville had shown that she appreciated the Seelbach. The guest list for the grand opening gala included Mr. and Mrs. Lawrence Jones of Anchorage, who had the largest party. The total number was 18 people. Other special guests were Mr. Jerry Fawcett of New Albany, Mr. and Mrs. J.D. Stewart and a party of 12 Messrs. W.L. Lyons, Harry Smyser and brother to J.L. Smyser, President of the Seelbach Realty Company, Marion E. Taylor, E.H. Bacon, and L.Y. Johnson.

Colonel Anderson Vennie of New York gave a dinner in honor of J.C.W. Beckman, Governor of Kentucky, who was the first to arrive. Harry J. Brennan and Matt J. Winn of Churchill Downs also attended. Mr. A.K. Cooper of Galt House fame and management confessed that he had come to mourn the Seelbach Hotel, but remained to rejoice.

His speech was a gem of generosity from a business rival and at its conclusion there was a rising acknowledgment of appreciation.

Grand Opening Menu

Mr. Charles T. Ballard introduced several citizens who gave an expression of the public's appreciation to Messrs. Louis and Otto Seelbach, "who by their enterprise and public spirit did aid in the development of the City of Louisville."

The menu for the evening consisted of Oyster Cocktail, Clear Green Turtle Soup in cups, Turbot of Black Bass, Dominicaine Potatoes, Gastronome, Venison Steak Louisianaise, Hot Asparagus Moderne, Punch L'Enferno, Quail sur Canapé, Champagne Cliquot Dry, topped off with cigarettes, cigars and some good Kentucky bourbon.

❧

The Ladies' Parlor, 1905

Ladies could not enter some restaurants, bars, hotels or government buildings without a male escort from about 1850 until the 1930s in Louisville. In that way, Louisville was no different from many of the big eastern cities—everything belonged to the gentlemen.

The name of the Seelbach's Gentleman's Bar & Grill stayed the same when the bar moved to Sixth and Main Streets. The Bar & Grill closed in 1885 and reopened in 1886 as the Seelbach Gentleman's Hotel. During these times, if a woman came to the bar or the hotel, she had to be escorted. But all hotels had Ladies' Parlors. If a gentleman were going to the billiards hall or to a meeting, the lady would wait in the Ladies' Parlor on the second floor.

■ *The Ladies' Parlor*

Death of a Salesman, 1906

(From newspaper reports)

On June 15, 1906, a New York lace dealer succumbs to pneumonia in Louisville, Kentucky. It was reported today that Louis Lee Zimmer, a member of the firm, J.F. Feeley and Company, lace dealers of New York, died at the Seelbach Hotel at 3:30 this afternoon. Death came three minutes after the arrival of T.J. Atchison, a business associate.

Mr. Zimmer came to Louisville about ten days ago and was stricken three days later. He sank gradually until two days ago, when Mr. Atchison was notified.

Mr. Zimmer was the son of Major General Zimmer, who was on General Robert E. Lee's staff at Appomattox. He was a member of the famous seventh regiment of New York. Louis Zimmer was

■ *The Lobby*

42 years old and is survived by his mother, who lives in New York. Mr. Atchison left for New York the same night with Mr. Zimmer's body.

Expansion, 1907

During the first two years, from 1905 to 1907, the hotel consisted of about 150 sleeping rooms.

The city was growing and the residential area was moving south, east and west. St. James Court was about to become the first big subdivision of Louisville. The Seelbach Realty Company was growing, along with the city. The company had already planned an expansion to the hotel. By January 1, 1907, the second phase of the hotel was completed. The hotel became a 500-room hotel of quiet elegance.

The addition of the north and south wings cost $300,000. This made the total cost of buying the property and construction $1,250,000. This addition gave the hotel a total of 225 bathrooms.

The hotel was ten stories tall and absolutely fireproof. The lower two floors were built of stone from Bowling Green, Kentucky and the remainder was built of Harvard Brick with stone trimmings.

Adding the two wings meant that the roof top garden would be treated differently than the old. It would be covered and enclosed, making it a winter garden as well.

■ *The Bavarian-style beer hall, the original Rathskeller.*

■ *The Seelbach Hotel upon completion of the expansion, 1907.*

■ *The Mezzanine, ca. 1910*

■ *The Gentlemen's Billiards Club, ca. 1910*

■ *The
Dining Room,
ca. 1910*

■ *The
Roof Garden,
ca. 1910*

■ *The expanded Seelbach Hotel, from a 1910 postcard.*

CHAPTER TWO

Presidents, Deaths,
and a New Owner

Two United States Presidents visited Louisville and stayed at the Seelbach Hotel. President William Howard Taft came to Louisville in April, 1911 for a brief visit. His home was in Cincinnati, Ohio. Taft spoke in the rooftop garden, which is no longer in existence.

President Woodrow Wilson arrived on September 4, 1916, to listen and talk to the people about their needs, as part of a whistlestop tour of the midwest.

The Great Wedding, 1918

Sometime in April, 1918, a young 2nd Lieutenant was going through Army training at Camp Taylor, located southeast of downtown Louisville, about eight miles from the Seelbach Hotel. The young officer had quit college to serve his country. He was a writer, and by this time he had written two short stories, but had not yet made it to the celebrity status he would enjoy later.

On weekend passes, he would visit the Seelbach, like so many other soldiers. After all, the Rathskeller was the USO during World War I. It was during three of his visits that, after an evening of bourbon and expensive cigars, he had to be restrained and kicked out of the hotel.

In 1918 the young lieutenant received his orders to be transferred to Ft. Sheridan in Montgomery, Alabama. It was during this time that he met his future wife, Zelda. They dated while he was at Fort Sheridan, became engaged, then broke it off for lack of money and the obligations of service.

In 1919 the lieutenant got out of the service and moved back to New York, which he called home. During the years between 1919 and 1922 he wrote several stories and even had a couple of books published.

He then went back to Montgomery and reunited with Zelda. They married a short time later. His journalistic talents got him a job in France in 1925. It was during that year that he remembered his days in Louisville and his evenings at the Seelbach. These memories enticed him to write the book for which he will always be remembered. The story was about a young couple—the woman from Louisville and the gentlemen from New York. They met and fell in love and married in the Grand Ballroom of the Seelbach Hotel. The couple's name in the Hotel registry was Tom and Daisy Buchanan—and the writer, the formerly young 2nd Lieutenant who caroused in the Seelbach Bar, as you may have surmised, was F. Scott Fitzgerald.

The Governor's Hot Bed, 1921

(From newspaper accounts)

A fire in room 741 early this morning at the Seelbach Hotel trapped Governor Edwin P. Morrow. Patrick Flynn, the head baggage man, rescued him.

According to the official report, Governor Morrow's bed caught fire from a lighted cigarette. The governor denied that he had been carried from his room, and immediately returned to Frankfort.

He said he awoke, found the bed on fire and called in men who extinguished it.

Patrick Flynn said that he was in the front of the hotel when he heard, "Help! Fire!" Looking up, he saw the Governor with his head out the window. "Don't jump! Hold steady!" Flynn called out. The head baggage man related how he obtained a pass key, ran to the Governor's room and rescued him.

—*The New York Times*, September 4, 1921.

A Day at the Races, 1921

Louis Seelbach was a member of the Board of Directors at Churchill Downs from 1914 until his death. His involvement with the track was so significant that the track named a race after the hotel for the fall meet.

On October 14, 1921, Marjorie Hynes, a filly running in the race for three-year-olds and upward, ran the best and captured the Seelbach Hotel Handicap at a mile with a field of four starters. The filly won by a length over Dr. Clark, while Rouleau was third, two lengths further back. Advocate was a distant fourth. Jockey Barnes rode Marjorie Hynes and she paid $5.70 to win.

The Seelbach Hotel Handicap changed names in the late 1920s.

No Limit Poker, 1923

The Kentucky Derby brings out the best horses, hats, people and now robbers. Derby Day, May 19, 1923, was no exception. Zev had won the Derby and the visitors were in a joyous mood, only to have the spell broken by a quartet of robbers.

Four soft-spoken armed bandits took $20,000 from twelve players in a poker game at the Seelbach Hotel.

A knock on the door announced the approach of the robbers. A spectator let the robbers into the crowded room. Four strangers entered with pistols in their right hands. "Keep your seats, gentlemen," the leader said. Then seeing the house detective in a corner, the leader instructed one of his followers to lock the officer in a closet. Wires to the room telephone were cut.

While three bandits pointed pistols at the spectators and players, a fourth searched each man, running his hands through pockets so deftly that several reported later they could not feel him frisking them. Locking the door and taking the key, the quartet left the hotel by the elevator and it is believed, mingled with Derby crowds on Louisville's streets. Police were unable to trace the robber's movements after leaving the lobby.

—*The New York Times*, May 19, 1923.

Louis Seelbach, Sr. Dies, 1925

The death of Louis Seelbach, Sr. on March 18, 1925 was a sad day for Louisville. Seelbach passed away in his apartment at the hotel. He was surrounded by his family at 8:00 p.m. when he succumbed to a yearlong battle with his illness.

Louis Seelbach was born in Rhenish, Bavaria, Germany on April 12, 1852. He came to Louisville at the age of 17, obtaining employment as one of the bellboys at the old Galt House Hotel at Second and Main streets. Mr. A.K. Cooper taught him everything he knew about the hotel business, and at the age of 22, Seelbach opened his first bar at Tenth and Main. Later he moved his bar to Sixth and Main. Otto Seelbach joined his brother in 1879 to open the Seelbach Bar and Grill. In 1891 they opened the first European Seelbach Hotel on the Sixth and Main site.

At the time of his death, Louis was president of the Seelbach Hotel Company. An interesting incident in Louis' life was his attendance several years before his death at the farewell banquet of his first employer, the old Galt House, given at the time of the announcement of its abandonment.

Louis Seelbach was survived by his wife, Mary Durbeck Seelbach; two sons, Louis Seelbach, Jr. and William O. Seelbach; a daughter, Mrs. Mary Helen Curtis of New York; and his brother and partner, Otto Seelbach.

Some of the most prominent guests Louis worked for and helped at social functions at the hotel were Presidents Theodore Roosevelt, William Howard Taft, and Warren G. Harding; General John J. Pershing; and David Lloyd George, former Prime Minister of England.

Chicago Man Buys the Seelbach, 1926

On April 1, 1926, publisher and real estate dealer Abraham M. Liebling bought the hotel from the Seelbach Realty Company. Mr. Liebling deposited $25,000 to close the deal which, according to members of the Seelbach Realty Company, involved approximately $2,500,000. The new owner signed the contract at a meeting in the office of John W. Barr, Jr., a member of the Realty firm.

■ *This was Louis Seelbach's office at the hotel. After his death, the office was converted into the Seelbach Suite, in which President Harry S. Truman stayed on September 30, 1948.*

Mr. Liebling left for Chicago Saturday night and announced that he would return the following week when the title was to be examined.

Jacob L. Smyser, President of the Realty Company, gave possession to Mr. Liebling on April 1, 1926. The sale of the Seelbach represented the largest individual real estate transaction in the history of Louisville.

Mr. Liebling came to the Kentucky Derby in 1925 and stayed at the Seelbach. He was the publisher of the *Jewish Daily Press* of Chicago.

The Depression

The Roaring '20s hit the Seelbach just as it had everything else and everyone in the United States. The hotel was sold twice during this time.

These are the memories of one of its employees during the '20s.

Mrs. Marjorie Thompson of Bardstown, Kentucky was working for Fulton and Fulton, a law firm during the early '20s. Business was slow, and someone had told her about the need for a secretary at the Seelbach Hotel, so she moved to Louisville.

Mrs. Thompson was recommended for the job, but being in her twenties she did not think she would get it. However, she did get the job working as the secretary for the General Manager, Mr. E.J. Moriarty.

The job consisted of a lot of paperwork for the general manager, but as Mrs. Thompson said, "It was not a difficult job," and she really enjoyed working at the hotel. She remembered the hotel being called a ritzy place and also a sinkhole by the news.

Mrs. Thompson remembered the hotel having some permanent

residents living in the apartments. One of those was Zack Jacobi, who had lived in the hotel since 1905.

Mrs. Thompson said, "The Seelbach was, and I guess still is now, a truly beautiful place with its huge and rustic look. You could see it from almost anywhere in Louisville. It was about ten stories high." Mrs. Thompson remembers "the socializing" with the fine people that worked for the hotel at the time.

The Kentucky Derby is one thing that never changes. All rooms are sold and on the day of the races, when everyone is gone to the track, you can hear a pin drop in the lobby and when it is over, let the party begin.

When the Depression hit Louisville, Mrs. Thompson lost her job at the hotel, but not her memories. They had to lay her off and hire a man who could type and also carry bags. That would not happen today, as some women can carry more than the men.

Several people were let go and the general manager told them to take any of the pictures from the hotel as they were going to remodel and get new ones. Mrs. Thompson took a small painting because she lived in an apartment and could not take a large one. Wherever Mrs. Thompson went, she took the painting with her. She said, "I think it is beautiful, just like the Seelbach." Mrs. Thompson still had the painting at the time of her death. It is now hanging in the home of Peggy Hill, the niece of Mrs. Thompson.

Otto Seelbach Dies, 1933

(From newspaper accounts)

Otto Seelbach, 1904 Village Drive, retired Vice President and Secretary of one of the most famous hostelries in the nation, died at 5:30 p.m. Monday, April 4, 1933, at St. Joseph's Infirmary. He was 70 years old.

Mr. Seelbach had been in failing health and underwent an operation on March 27. He was the last of three brothers to immigrate to America from their native country, Germany. Otto Seelbach is survived by his wife, Bertha Seelbach, daughter J. Durry Hancock and son, Otto E. Seelbach.

The Rathskeller Re-opens, 1934

On April 20, 1934, the Rathskeller reopened with a 56-foot bar attended by six bartenders at 9:00 p.m. on a Saturday night. A noted room in pre-Prohibition days, the Rathskeller's new opening featured special entertainment and a floorshow. The Ray Ash Band furnished music.

Improvements in the decoration and appointments of the Rathskeller were made preparatory to the new opening. Waitresses dressed in Bavarian costumes accentuated the Bavarian atmosphere in the Rathskeller. The renovations were made under the supervision of James A. Hickey.

More Presidents, 1938

President Franklin D. Roosevelt made an overnight campaign visit to the Seelbach on July 8, 1938.

© The Courier-Journal

■ *President Franklin D. Roosevelt (far left), A.B. "Happy" Chandler (middle), and Vice-President Alben Barkley ride in a motorcade together.*

Angeline at the Seelbach

Beginning in the 1920s, author Cordia Greer-Petrie wrote a long-running series of books called *Angeline at the Seelbach*, featuring a young country girl named Angeline from the hills of Eastern Kentucky, coming to the city of Louisville and the Seelbach Hotel.

Mrs. Petrie grew up in Merry Oaks in Barren County. She was educated in Louisville's public schools and Eminence College.

Sweet Angeline made her first visit to Louisville and the Seelbach Hotel in 1921. Angeline and Lum went to Louisville with Jedge Bowles, who "tuck 'm round to the Seelbach Hotel." The comic novels derive their humor from Angeline's encounters in the big city, such as in this passage: "I felt sorter backerd about bein' around thar, bekaze we uns didn't know any of them Seelback's and I shore hated to go in on 'em without lettin 'em know we wuz a-comin. I'd always thought the Phoenix Hotel up at the county seat wuz some punkins, but sakes alive, hit ain't a patchin' to Miss Seelback's place."

Mrs. Petrie was a pioneer of the airwaves, having appeared in 1923 on the new-fangled WHAS Radio phone. The Petries had no children, "only my brain child, Angeline," said Mrs. Petrie.

ANGELINE
at the
SEELBACH
by
Cordia Greer-Petrie

■ *The Seelbach Bar was the preeminent watering hole of Louisville before Prohibition, and regained its status after Prohibition was repealed.*

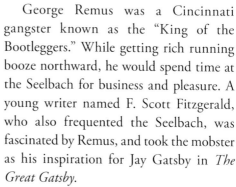

George Remus was a Cincinnati gangster known as the "King of the Bootleggers." While getting rich running booze northward, he would spend time at the Seelbach for business and pleasure. A young writer named F. Scott Fitzgerald, who also frequented the Seelbach, was fascinated by Remus, and took the mobster as his inspiration for Jay Gatsby in *The Great Gatsby.*

Other infamous mob types drawn to Louisville during Prohibition included Lucky Luciano, Al Capone and Dutch Schultz.

CHAPTER THREE

Into the Modern Era

Zack Jacoby, 1905–1950

Man Who Moved Into the Seelbach Hotel the Day It Opened, Still Lives There. Zack Jacoby Surpasses Ripley Record

Zack Jacoby moved into the Seelbach opening day, May 1, 1905, and he has been there ever since. That is believed to be a record for Ripley's Believe It or Not, for years living in a hotel, surpassing the 41 years by a Los Angeles man.

It was his civic pride and determination not to let the Los Angeles man get ahead of him, or Louisville, that induced Jacoby to permit his name to be mentioned in a newspaper. Mr. Jacoby said he loves the Seelbach, where he has lived for nearly 44 years. Mr. Jacoby was an executive for Kaufman-Strauss Company for 37 years before his retirement 24 years ago. He is a bachelor.

As for the Seelbach, where he lives in a spacious, quiet room with books, a radio and numerous photographs, he recalled how Louis and Otto Seelbach were criticized for going out in the wilderness to build a hotel. That location was considered by many to be too far removed from the busy Main Street.

—*The Courier-Journal*, February 27, 1949

Opening Day Guest at Seelbach In 1905 Dies.
Zack Jacoby stayed at the hotel for 45 years.

On Saturday, January 31, 1953, Zack Jacoby died at a nursing home at 1371 Overbacker Court. Jacoby moved into the Seelbach Hotel the day it opened in 1905 and lived there until he went into the nursing home three years ago. A bachelor, Jacoby was in his 80s.

Loaded Suitcase, 1950s

On December 6, 2004, this story was told to the lobby concierge:

A 76 year-old gentleman stated he had been a bellman at the Seelbach Hotel during the 1950s. He remembered helping a guest to his room late one night. The guest had two suitcases and a briefcase.

When they arrived at his room, the bellman got the luggage racks from the closet and put the suitcases on them. The bellman then checked the room to make sure everything was proper. After doing this, he gave the guest the room key and went back to the bell stand.

Two weeks later the general manager called the bellman to his office. When the bellman arrived at his office, there were two other men waiting with the general manager. The two men were police officers. They wanted to know about the man who checked into room 766 two weeks earlier. The bellman told them that nothing was strange, but his suitcases were very heavy, and that it seemed like he wanted the bellman out of the room quickly. He had tipped him $20.

The two police officers told the general manager and the bellman that the bags were full of money. The man had robbed a bank earlier in the day.

✤

Different Owners, 1929–1975

The Seelbach Hotel was sold on several occasions during the period 1929–1956.

Abraham Liebling bought the hotel from the Seelbach brothers for $2,500,000 in 1926.

In 1929, after managing the hotel for several years, the Eppley Company bought the hotel for $2,000,000. During these years, Eppley purchased 18 other hotels throughout the Midwest, including the Hotel Fontenelle in Omaha.

The year 1956 brought many changes to the Seelbach Hotel. The Eppley Company sold all of its hotels to the Sheraton Hotel Corporation for about $30,000,000. The value of the Seelbach purchase was not announced. Even though Eppley sold the hotels to Sheraton, they became a division of Sheraton and managed 22 of the hotels.

Sheraton came in and remodeled (modernized) the guest rooms, meeting rooms and restaurants of the hotel.

The Sheraton's lobby modernization was acceptable by 1950s standards, but a tragedy by today's preservation standards. The company put a drop ceiling just below the murals, paneled the columns, painted the walls, and put red linoleum on the marble floor. It stayed this way until 1970.

Sheraton soon renamed the hotel the Sheraton-Seelbach, and later changed it to just The Sheraton. The citizens of Louisville, especially the ones attuned to preservation and tradition, were upset at this news.

In 1968, Sheraton sold the Seelbach and the Watterson Hotel to the Gotham Corporation of New York for $3,800,000.

In 1969, Gotham gave Louisville back the Seelbach name and the following year, under the guidance of Allen Goldman, son of the owner of Gotham Hotels, the drop ceiling was removed and the murals uncovered. The ceiling workers responsible for removing the paneling from the murals damaged the peasant farmer worker.

In 1975, Gotham went bankrupt which, combined with the deterioration of downtown and tourist flight to suburban hotels, caused the Seelbach to close its doors for seven years.

The Plantation Room, 1941

The drugstore that had been associated with the Seelbach Hotel for almost 20 years moved in 1941. In its place the hotel opened a nightclub called the Plantation Room.

The club featured dining and dancing for patrons. There was a 25-foot-wide diorama on the main wall facing Walnut Street and a glass-enclosed staircase going from the main floor to the balcony.

The hotel kept a private entrance into the club for its overnight guests, and the Walnut Street entrance for other guests. The Plantation Room was the first dinner-dancing nightclub in Louisville.

During the early 1960s, the Plantation Room closed and became the Blue Boar Cafeteria. The room still had charm and beauty, the same as its sister property.

 The Plantation Room

The cafeteria became a Louisville tradition and a place for downtown workers to eat lunch at a fair price. Despite its success at lunchtime, the cafeteria did not do much business at night, and the cafeteria closed in the mid 1970s.

The room was used for storage after the Seelbach reopened in 1982.

⚜

Lady Bouncer, 1944

Jitterbugging juveniles during World War II didn't dare darken the doorways of the several taverns operated by the Seelbach Hotel, and the reason was a tall, dark, handsome, six- foot woman everyone called the "Lady Bouncer."

With so many men off fighting in the war, Miss Vera Guy, 25, night after night patrolled the hotel's parlors where alcoholic drinks were served. In her time at the hotel she sent literally thousands of underage girls, sailors, marines and soldiers on their way.

Miss Guy used a friendly smile and pleasing manner to accomplish her task of bouncer. Not once did she have to use her 185 pounds to enforce a decision. Very few juveniles put up an argument. If they had been served drinks before they got to the hotel, they may have tried to protest. But Miss Guy quickly convinced them it was useless.

On weekends the hotel had seven male house detectives on the job, but never once was Miss Guy compelled to call a man to her assistance.

Air Conditioning, 1947

Since 1916, the Seelbach Hotel had had a public utility franchise to sell steam, and furnished heat to several downtown buildings as well as the hotel.

In 1947, the hotel installed steam air-conditioning in a 30-foot square space, becoming the first building to be air-conditioned in the city of Louisville. The cost was $350,000. The system cooled over half of the 500 rooms within a year. The water for the steam mechanism came from two wells under the hotel. According to the general manager at the time, J. R. Gaughenbauch, the Seelbach was the only hotel in the midwest that had steam-operated air-conditioning. The system changed air in the rooms every five minutes, and occupants could adjust room temperature by turning a knob resembling a knob on a radio receiving set.

The President Slept Here, September 30, 1948

The Seelbach welcomed President and Mrs. Harry Truman to the hotel on September 30, 1948.

The Trumans stayed in room 940, the State Suite. Before they even arrived, the suite was renamed the Presidential Suite, and was known by that name from then on.

The Presidential Suite once was the private office and quarters of the Louis Seelbach family (see page 43).

The Presidential Suite's bedroom was decorated in bright wallpaper and on the beds were antique, dark emerald-colored satin spreads. Originally this room had had leather walls and dark woodwork.

Mrs. Truman and her daughter Margaret's bedroom was decorated more on the feminine side. The furniture was covered in pale green and pink satin. Lampshades on the dresser were white with ruffles.

Simon Maker, who had been a waiter with the hotel for 40 years, served evening meals in the suite.

The entire Ninth floor was taken by the President, his family, 75 newspapermen and others traveling with the President.

In 1982 the Presidential Suite was renamed the Seelbach Suite, and room 930 was expanded and named the Presidential Suite.

A Movie at the Hotel, 1959

Glitter and stars invaded the hotel in 1959. The movie industry was in Louisville, and at the Seelbach, to shoot scenes for a movie called "The Hustler." The stars were Jackie Gleason and Paul Newman playing pool hustlers "Minnesota Fats" and "Fast Eddie" Felson.

The billiards hall on the mezzanine level of the Seelbach was a perfect location for pool-shooting scenes since it was called the best in the midwest.

But only one billiards scene was shot in the hall; the rest were shot at Westminster Hall in New York.

President Johnson, 1964

President and Mrs. Lyndon Johnson visited Louisville in 1964, on the campaign trail for Vice President Hubert H. Humphrey.

■ *Lady Bird Johnson shakes hands with a large crowd of Humphrey supporters gathered in front of the Seelbach Hotel in 1964.*

The Seelbach Closes, 1975

The bankruptcy of the Seelbach's owners could not have come at a worse time. Louisville's once-vibrant downtown was back on its heels in 1975, reeling from the movement of the population to the suburbs and the subsequent loss of retail businesses and services in the city center. The hotel was forced to close. The *Courier-Journal* wrote the following two articles to lament the situation.

No Place to Stay

The once luxurious hotels of downtown are closing. The Brown Hotel in 1971, The Kentucky Hotel in 1973, The Watterson earlier this year and now the Seelbach.

A night time visit to 4th and Walnut is strange, almost as if the Seelbach sign knows. The "S" and "E" in the vertical sign looming over the corner, flickered between pink and white. The "E", "L" and "B" had already faded into a sort of ivory frieze, emanating no light. The final three letters of "Seelbach" burned strong, forming in big red letters "ACH" as if in pain from its closing in the next few days.

Such a sign would be fitting because "ACH" in German is the utterance for surprises, sadness or disgust.

The Seelbach will probably close this week. As of tomorrow, June 26, 1975, the Seelbach hotel would have been open 70 years, two months and 26 days.

The general manager, Pat Cleary, and Gotham representatives, tried to stop the closing in hopes of turning it into the "Seelbach Dormitory" but it fell through.

The cab stand was a busy place at 4th and Walnut, said one of the cab drivers. "I used to get lots of business here, the convention people were always wanting to go somewhere."

The Seelbach hotel served its country working with the army to house draftees before they went to basic training during World War II and the Korean War.

In a 1954 incident, six soldiers-to-be from Grant County carpeted their Seelbach room knee-deep in feathers in order to be arrested and thereby delay their induction.

A boiler room engineer said he was hired two months ago and Sunday would be his last day. He said he wanted experience and then it was all over. He was unemployed again.

A bellman and Seelbach veteran of 25 years said he had known all along that the hotel would close. Two soldiers from Ft. Knox, when told of the news, shrugged their shoulders and said, "Guess we'll have to find another place to stay on the 4th of July."

Memories, 1977

The Seelbach has been closed for about 16 months and the memories linger on. The hotel was like a mirage, a jewel in the Nile, or a ray of sunshine, as some of the older workers from days gone by would say.

Six former Presidents visited the Seelbach—William Howard Taft, who spoke on the rooftop garden, which is no longer there; Woodrow Wilson; Franklin D. Roosevelt; Harry Truman; John F. Kennedy; and Lyndon Johnson. An oak-paneled marble bathroom adorned the presidential suite on the 9th floor and was re-designed in 1948 for Truman's whistle stop campaign in Kentucky. It had been the private quarters for Louis Seelbach's family.

Some people remembered the view from the roof top garden on

the 10th floor. The majestic panoramic view of the Ohio River and the Indiana shore.

There was a Georgian Gentleman's Café designed after a room in Hampton Court Palace in England, and the Rathskeller, where stars from the McCauley Theater dined. It is the only remaining example of a room decorated entirely with tiles from Rookwood Pottery in Cincinnati, Ohio.

Singer Gerardi Floreatine's Orchestra occupied the musician's gallery and entertained with such hit tunes as, "Piff Paff Pouf" and "Rufus Rastas Johnson Brown, What you going to do when the rent comes around."

Lillian Russell was among the famous people who stayed at the hotel when she was appearing in a musical version of "She Stoops To Conquer" at McCauley's Theater. Louisville's Cordia Greer Petrie wrote a book entitled *Angeline at the Seelbach*. She also stayed at the Seelbach.

In the later years the hotel had a restaurant known as the "Stables" with a horse motif and the Plantation Room had a moving diorama that included a tooting steamboat.

F. Scott Fitzgerald visited the hotel when he was stationed at Camp Taylor in 1918 and wrote about it in *The Great Gatsby* in 1925.

The hotel, which has been as much a part of Louisville as the Ohio River, is listed on the National Register of Historic Places and has been designated a Kentucky Landmark.

CHAPTER FIVE

Roger Davis and the New Dream, 1978

The dream of bringing the Seelbach Hotel back from the dead began in 1978. On December 28, 1978, Roger Davis, a native Louisvillian who made a name for himself as a TV actor in Hollywood, and Gil Whittenberg Jr., a Louisville construction company owner, announced their plans for restoring the Louisville landmark.

They purchased the hotel for between $800,000 and $1 million, and embarked on a trip into something of the unknown, just as the Seelbach brothers had done 70 years earlier.

The hotel had been closed and abandoned since 1975, and deterioration had set in quickly. Paint chips were hanging from the ceiling, the walls had holes in them, and vinyl covered the original marble floor in the lobby.

Renovation work got overwhelming quickly.

Davis' and Whittenberg Jr.'s overall plan was to restore the hotel to its original grandeur, uncovering the marble, lobby frescoes and classical woodwork that had been covered by drywall during the Sheraton's period of ownership. The specific plan was to take the hotel's 460 rooms and turn them into 300–325 larger ones. An indoor pool was also planned.

■ *The big dreamer on the Seelbach renovation team was Roger Davis, whose enthusiasm and stubbornness to recreate the hotel to its original grandeur were mostly responsible for its ultimate success.*

Most of the guest rooms were to have four-poster beds and tall armoires and be decorated in a combination of paper and fabric. Hallways would feature wooden molding and marble, and the ceilings were to be raised a foot.

The city agreed to build a parking garage behind the hotel for 1000 cars.

Windows of the Past

Jerome B. Pound from Chattanooga, Tennessee designed, built and owned the Henry Watterson Hotel, across from the Seelbach Hotel. It was a ten-story structure with some great treasures, just like the Seelbach.

The Henry Watterson opened in 1912 and was a great success. By the early '20s, the Seelbach Realty Company had bought the Henry Watterson Hotel and it remained part of a package deal with the Seelbach Hotel.

In 1978, Roger Davis bought both hotels, knowing the Henry Watterson would be downtown. The city was trying to revive downtown Louisville and the twin towers and the Galleria were going to be built on part of the property. The Henry Watterson Hotel, like the Seelbach, was a historical site and in order to tear it down, parts of the hotel would have to be put in some other building, so it could live on.

The construction company saved the stain glass windows from the ballroom and eventually they were put in the foyer of the Seelbach's Grand Ballroom.

The center window was a complete mystery until May, 2006.

The window on the left is the shield of the City of Louisville. On the right is the shield of Kentucky. Those windows were self-explained by the inscriptions on them.

It was discovered in May 2006 that the center window represents the Royal Arms of the United Kingdom of Great Britain and Northern Ireland. It was one of the most familiar heraldic emblems

in the English-speaking world and dates back to 1857, when Queen Victoria was crowned. The symbols have been modified as late as 1957, four years after Queen Elizabeth II took the throne.

The Royal Arms is divided into four quarters. Two represent England, one is for Scotland and one is for Ireland. The three golden lions and the red rose—England; the pacing red lion and pink thistle—Scotland; and the silver gold harp on a bright blue field and shamrock—Ireland.

The shield is circled with a blue ribbon of the order of the Garter, carrying in gold letters the motto of Britain's most exclusive society, *Honi Soit Qui Mal y Pense*, which means, "Blame to him who thinks evil of it." The Royal British lion and the silver Scotch unicorn support the design on either side.

At the bottom of the arms is the royal motto in gold letters on a white scroll, "*Dieu et mon Droit*," which means, "God and my right" (a fuller version of the motto is also quoted as "God and my right shall me defend").

The crown at the top was used in the coronation ceremonies of Queen Elizabeth II.

■ *Ongoing renovation.*

❧

"Stripes," 1979

The first of four movies shot at the Seelbach in the late 1970s and early 1980s began during the fall of 1979.

The movie was called "Stripes"and was, at the time, a small-budget feature with a cast of young, relatively unknown comic actors—Bill Murray, Harold Ramis, John Candy, John Larroquette, Judge Reinhold and Sean Young (a native Louisvillian). All went on, of course, to become big-time stars in television and movies, but

■ *Author Larry Johnson on the set with "Stripes" star Bill Murray.*

in 1979 they went about their business on the streets of downtown Louisville without much fanfare. The film is about a bunch of misfits going through Army basic training at Ft. Arnold (Ft. Knox). One of the scenes in the movie was shot at the corner of Fourth and Muhammad Ali in front of the Seelbach during reconstruction. Most of the movie was shot within 35 miles of Louisville.

❧

Fire, October 15, 1981

On October 15, 1981, a fire ravaged part of the Seelbach Hotel. The cause of the fire was attributed to renovations that were underway at the hotel. The fire caused more than $50,000 in damage, most of it to about 100 marble pedestal sinks that were shattered by the heat.

The fire apparently started when a worker's blowtorch ignited cardboard boxes containing the sinks. The hotel suffered little damage and did not disrupt its commitment to reopen in March, 1982.

The Lobby

To Roger Davis and Gil Whittenberg, new owners of the Seelbach, restoration of the lobby was the most sensitive and most important part of redoing the hotel. Under their plan, the lobby would be about 75% restored to its original state, or as close to the 1905 original as humanly possible.

The task turned out to be daunting. The frieze/fresco of the peasant farmers on the lobby walls that had been destroyed in 1970 by workers had to be replaced. The area had been re-plastered and a copy of the Indian Chief was hung in the farmers' place. Sixteen

■ *The Lobby Stairs*

coats of paint were discovered on the walls, and three layers of wallpaper had to be steamed off the marble.

A red linoleum sheet had been placed on the lobby's original marble, which had come from Italy, France, Germany, Switzerland and Alabama. When it was removed, the beautiful floor was destroyed and had to be replaced.

In the early years the lobby had been lighted by small chandeliers, wall lamps, and the 900-panel glass skylight. The skylight was found to be beyond repair during the restoration and was covered by a metal fabrication. The small chandeliers were replaced by large chandeliers recovered from the Phoenix Hotel of Lexington, Kentucky. (The hotel's proprietor from 1905 to 1920 had been Charles Seelbach, Louis and Otto Seelbach's younger brother.)

The front desk was too small for the new lobby configuration, and was replaced by a beautifully carved and constructed masterpiece.

March 26, 1982–Trial Run

Most of the staff of the Seelbach were called to work on March 10, 1982, in anticipation of the grand opening later in the month. Management wanted to give the hotel a trial run to get the inevitable kinks out of the system. On March 26, the hotel opened its first 45 rooms. The hotel's general manager, Thomas Payne, who had opened other hotels, said, "All 45 rooms are reserved for Seelbach corporate staff and some paying customers."

The brand-new hotel had 324 rooms with rates ranging from $56 to $350 for the Presidential Suite. The hotel was sold out for six months ahead of the Kentucky Derby in May.

One of the early customers was a writer with the *Courier-Journal*. He wanted to help open the Seelbach and at the same time do a story. He pulled up to the front door of the hotel to see a doorman in a top hat and tails.

The doorman tried getting the luggage from the back seat of the car three different times, bumping his head each time. He tried with his right hand, holding his top hat in place with his left, and then switched, and neither worked. Finally he hunkered down and reached fully into the back seat with both hands. It was a learning experience for him as well as the rest of the staff.

Snags, April, 1982

After the Seelbach opened for a trial run for a few overnight guests, the hotel had problems with some of its fire safety systems. The hotel planned to open officially on April 12, 1982, and in April it tried to finish what needed to be done to get its certificate of occupancy from the city of Louisville.

With its fire safety system incomplete, the hotel had to hire ten firefighters, one positioned on each floor in case of fire, to direct the guests during the Preservation Ball, which was attended by 800 people. Roger Davis said he would pick up the $3,200 tab for the firefighters' overtime pay.

 This movie set for "Bless 'em All" was established in front of the Seelbach.

❖

A Movie, 1982

Two days before the Grand Opening Gala, the movie industry moved in to shoot scenes for a movie called "Bless 'em All," which involved a hotel robbery in the Roaring '20s.

The stars were Eddie Albert and Jill St. John. Several scenes took place in the hotel as well as on the street in front of the hotel.

Grand Opening, 1982

With all the training and anticipation of the Grand Opening, the night did not let anyone down.

© The Courier-Journal

■ *On a Seelbach balcony, the American flag was unfurled while the band played "My Old Kentucky Home" during the Grand Opening ceremonies.*

The doormen were decked out in tails, top hats and white gloves. The bellmen were dressed in black jackets and pants, white shirts and pin-striped aprons.

The front desk looked like something out of *Architectural Digest*. It was a beautiful setting for a big night.

The lobby was decorated with flowers and a big champagne fountain in the middle of the floor. The bell stand was located by the Old Seelbach Bar.

There were about 1000 invited guests and hundreds of bystanders on the street who came to see what celebrities might arrive. Television cameras and newspaper reporters were everywhere.

The first limo I dealt with arrived about 7:00 p.m. I went to the door and said everything I was trained to say. The person stepping out was a beautiful young lady. I was speechless. The driver of the limo said, "This is . . ." and before she could give me her real name, I said, "Hope Spalding of Guiding Light." My daughter and I watched that television show together. Ms. Spalding came back out front later,

■ *A large crowd gathered outside the Seelbach Hotel for the official reopening of the Louisville landmark.*

and I continued to call her "Hope." That was the start of a long list of celebrities at the Seelbach.

Baseball, 1982

Professional baseball came back to Louisville in the same year the Seelbach reopened. Mr. A. Ray Smith, the new owner of the Louisville Redbirds, stayed at the Seelbach during the opening week of play. He held a press conference in front of the hotel and at the end of his talk said, "Let's play ball!"

A crowd of 19,632 cheered professional baseballs' return to Louisville. No one seemed to mind the bitter cold that April night, or that the Redbirds lost, 7 to 4.

Democrats, 1982

In 1982 the Democratic Party returned to the Seelbach Hotel for the first time since 1971. The hotel had been the official headquarters of the party from 1947 to 1971.

Governor Earle Clements was the one who started staying in the hotel in 1947, during his gubernatorial campaign. The reservation desk gave him room 743.

Election day in 1947 saw Earle Clements win the governor's race, and he let it be known that his success was because of lucky room 743. For the next 24 years, Democrats stayed in that room while strategizing and planning their campaigns.

The most notable Democrats to visit room 743 were Bert Combs and Ned Breathitt. Both became governors in later years.

In 1982 there was a reunion of what the Democrats called "The 743 Club." Attending were more than 200 candidates, chairmen, elected officials and grassroots party workers from dozens of bygone campaigns.

Everyone who attended reminisced about the many years of campaigning in the hotel. The ones who brought smiles to everyone's faces were Governor Ned Breathitt with his song, "Hey look me over" and Governor Happy Chandler's, "Happy days are here again."

The hotel associate recognized during the reunion for his hard work for the Democratic Party was Martin "Brownie" Brown, the credit manager at the Seelbach during the era. Brownie attended the reunion with his wife and advised that "he had the job of deciding who got room 743."

Also recognized were Pat Cleary, the manager of the hotel, and Miss Frankye Scott, the hotel's reservation manager.

Stories from a Doorman, 1982–1983

Shortly after the grand opening, an elderly couple came by the front of the hotel. The lady was in her 80's. She told the doorman about how she and her husband had spent the first night of their honeymoon at the Seelbach. She went on to say that her husband had been upset because the room rate was so high. The nightly rate in those years was $2. The next day they had moved to the Berkley Hotel down the street for only $1 a night.

The doorman jokingly asked if they still had their receipt, and a few months later the couple returned with the 60-year-old receipt in hand. The front desk manager gave them a room for $2, but told them they had to use it on their anniversary night. The couple checked in and the next day the lady came to thank the doorman for his kindness. Her husband was upset again. He had only paid $2 for the room, but had to pay $8 for parking. He was still a tightwad.

The second story comes from a woman walking on Fourth Street in front of the hotel. A gentleman was walking ahead of the lady. They were both admiring the hotel. When she stopped to ask about the Rathskeller, she commented that she had some great times during World War I dancing with the young soldiers from Camp Taylor, when the Rathskeller was the USO club.

The doorman asked her if she wanted to go down and see the Rathskeller room again. She replied, "No thanks, I want to remember it the way it was, when I met my first true love down there." The doorman asked if it was the gentleman she was with. Her response was, "Heck no, I was married to him and he was off fighting the war."

■ *The 600 block of the Fourth Avenue Mall, 1982.*

Cat Thief

Derby Day weekend, 1983, brought thieves of all kinds to Louisville—pickpockets, armed robbers, embezzlers and cat thieves.

On the Friday before Derby, Eunice Davis went to bed around midnight. She told the police that she was sure the door was firmly locked from the inside.

When Mrs. Davis awoke, she called security and they notified the police department that a thief had entered her room and stolen jewelry with an estimated value of at least $500,000.00. The police said this is probably the largest heist in Louisville hotel history.

Roger Davis (no relation), the Seelbach's CEO, said it takes a special key to unlock a deadbolt lock and there are only two keys. He also said, "It's intriguing as to how this was accomplished." The commander of the crime unit for the Louisville police said there was no sign of forced entry at the door or the windows of Mrs. Davis' tenth floor room. Mrs. Davis did not hear or see anything.

The theft from Mrs. Davis' room was not the only loss from the Seelbach reported that night. Joseph O'Neill from Midland, Texas reported over $600,000 in jewelry stolen from his third floor room. Again, the police commented that there was no sign of forced entry. Everyone had questions about what happened:

How did the thief or thieves get into the rooms?

Is there a connection between the two thefts?

Were hotel employees involved?

Could it have been sophisticated thieves who came to Louisville, especially to work the money-laden Kentucky Derby crowd?

We will probably never know who or how these thefts happened during the Derby weekend of 1983.

—*This story was taken in part from the May 13, 1983* Courier-Journal.

Miss Piggy, 1983

Jim Henson's *Muppets On Ice* was to appear at the Fairgrounds. A few days before the show, the Miss Piggy character was doing a promotion with the Seelbach Hotel.

The assistant general manager of the hotel, Vinnie Gupta, came to me and said that Miss Piggy would be arriving by convertible and that I was to help her get out of the car and lead her into the hotel. Miss Piggy would then go through the lobby and go out the back door and back to the Holiday Inn.

The car pulled up and I greeted her with a tilt of my top hat. I opened the door with my left hand. Miss Piggy put her paw in my hand to balance herself and, without thinking, I kissed her paw.

The next day Miss Piggy and I were in the newspaper, with me kissing her paw.

Preferred Hotel, 1983

In 1983, only one year after its grand reopening, the Seelbach was designated one of the elite hotels in the world. The Preferred Hotel Group's board met in Zurich, Switzerland and notified the Seelbach's Chief Executive Officer, Roger Davis, of their selection.

At the time there were only 40 hotels in the elite category.

About 20 hotels in the United States were members of the elite association.

The Lady in the Mirror, 1983

Until 1986, Otto's Café, on the first floor, was smaller than it is today. There was a wall in place of the columns and mirrors down the north and south walls. The café opened at 6:00 a.m. and closed at midnight.

In December, 1983, there was a young man cleaning up in the café. His job was to vacuum the carpets, wash the mirrors and tables and anything that needed to be done to get the café ready for the next day. While cleaning the tables, he glanced into the mirrors on the south wall and saw an old lady in ragged clothes and an orange floppy hat. He thought she was a street person, and he was going to let her warm up while he cleaned. He saw her several times and finally, when he turned to tell her she would have to leave, she was not there. He looked in the mirror again and saw her, but when he turned around, she was gone. The young man called security, who checked the hotel from top to bottom. No street person was found.

The next year there was a different person cleaning the café, and the lady was seen again in the mirror. The head of security checked the logbook and discovered that the two sightings had occurred on the same day and at almost the same time, one year apart.

There is no information about anyone dying in that café, but over the years the area had been a bar, a restaurant, an office and a storage room.

The lady with the orange floppy hat has never been seen since. However, if you ever sit inside the door on the left and your food disappears, don't worry, she does not eat much.

Sold, 1984

Roger Davis and Gil Whittenberg, who resurrected the Seelbach from a sorry state in 1978, sold their 50% share of the hotel to the Metropolitan Insurance Company, which had owned the other half since 1979. The company paid $12.7 million to Old Seelbach Inc.

Metropolitan pledged to maintain the luxury status and service of the historic, 322-room hotel and said that the National Hotel Corporation would continue to manage the Seelbach.

■ *The Seelbach's front entrance at Fourth Street and Muhammad Ali Blvd.*

CHAPTER SIX

Ghosts, Gangsters, and Gorbachev

❧

The Lady in Blue, 1936

This is a brief look into the story of Patricia Wilson, the "Lady in Blue."

During Sunday brunch one hot July day in 1987, two separate hotel associates saw a woman in a blue dress walk into the elevator—with the doors closed. The first sighting occurred on the hotel's Mezzanine level and the other on the eighth floor.

James Scott was cooking waffles for Sunday brunch on the Mezzanine. He looked out toward the small elevators and saw a dark-haired lady in a blue dress walk into the elevator through closed doors. Shaken, he called a security guard who checked the elevator and could find nothing.

A short time later a housekeeper on the eighth floor saw a lady go into the same elevator in the same manner. The security guard, called again, talked with both associates and found that their descriptions of the lady were identical.

The apparition remained a mystery until 1992, when Alex Hunt discovered an article in the 1936 newspaper about the death of a woman in a Seelbach elevator.

It seems that a young couple had just moved to Louisville from

Oklahoma. The Wilsons had been married for four years but had separated. Mrs. Patricia Wilson was 24 years old and lived at 847 South First Street.

Their landlady had said, "The Wilsons were trying to work things out and they planned a meeting at the Seelbach. Mr. Wilson was killed in a car wreck on his way to the hotel. A few nights later, Patricia fell to her death in a dark service elevator in the back of the Seelbach. She had a blue dress on."

So add The Lady in Blue to the list of ghosts who frequent the hotel.

The story became fairly well known nationally. On Halloween night, 2003, the Lady in Blue was a clue on "Jeopardy."

FALL VICTIM

MRS. PATRICIA WILSON.

GIRL LOSES LIFE IN HOTEL SHAFT

Coroner Delays Verdict As Body Found Atop Seelbach Elevator.

DEAD SEVERAL HOURS

Mrs. Patricia Wilson, 24, of 847 S. First, was found dead shortly before 8 a.m. Wednesday, lying atop a service elevator at the bottom of a shaft at the Seelbach Hotel.

◼ *The Lady in Blue was seen walking into this elevator in 1987. She had died in 1936, having fallen down this elevator shaft in the hotel.*

❖

Patricia or Lucy

This story was sent to me on April 16, 2006 from Margaret Bateman, the Kentucky Department of Tourism, Communication Branch.

Mrs. Bateman gave her father the first edition of this book. When she later visited him in Ohio, he said he thought he knew the Lady in Blue.

The following are Mr. Bateman's memories.

My dad (now 93 years old) was a member of the 107th mounted troop in Cleveland before the war started. In 1935, the troop was at Fort Knox for its two-week active duty training and he and his three friends went to Louisville for some "fun." (He told me he probably should not be telling this story, but he was single at the time.) They asked where the excitement was and were directed to Fifth Street. They went to a "house" and the madam brought them four girls. One of them was a knock-out and they called her "Lucy." The next year, they were back at Fort Knox and went back to the same house. They asked about Lucy and were told she had died in an elevator accident at the Seelbach. So now, we know how the "Lady in Blue" was making her living during the time she and her husband were separated. Her death may not have been an accident. Anyway, this sounds like a story for the TV show, "Cold Case."

This story was shared in memory of Margaret Bateman's father, who died April 22, 2006.

Larry Johnson, 1988 Hotel & Motel Association National Bellman

March of 1988 brought notoriety and publicity to the Seelbach Hotel. Larry Johnson, the Bell Captain, had been named The National Bellman of the Year.

The hotel was exposed to magazines and newspapers from the entire country, as well as on "Good Morning America" on ABC.

Good Morning America did a live interview with Mr. Johnson in the lobby on April 19th.

William O. Seelbach Jr. Dies, 1988

The grandson of Louis Seelbach died Friday in Boynton Beach, Florida. He was 71. His father, William O. Seelbach Sr., worked at the Seelbach Hotel for his father, Louis, and Uncle Otto Seelbach until 1933, when Otto passed away.

William O. Seelbach Jr.'s survivors include his wife, the former Elizabeth Simonds, two daughters, Anne Seelbach of Jersey City, NJ and two grandchildren.

Mr. Seelbach was laid to rest in Cave Hill Cemetery in Louisville, Kentucky.

John Young, October 23, 1899–May 20, 1989

80+ year-old John Young came out of retirement in 1982 to work as the bellman on the 11:00 p.m. to 7:00 a.m. shift at the Seelbach Hotel.

The story Mr. Young told the bell staff was that his wife Heloise, 81, was reading the Sunday newspaper when he told her he was going to hop bells again (be a bellman). Her reaction was, "You're too old!"

Well, he wasn't. Mr. Young worked with the hotel for six years before he got ill and had to retire again.

In 1987 John Young was named Bellman of the Year for the state of Kentucky.

❧

SWAT, 1990

Guests on the sixth floor of the Seelbach Hotel were surprised in 1990 when they came out of their rooms to see police officers in SWAT uniforms hustling them around the corner out of harm's way.

It seems a guest in room 620 was barricaded in his room, threatening to blow up the hotel with a hand grenade. He said he also had a machine gun.

The officers were able to get the man out without anyone getting injured. The officers said that they did not think he ever had the weapons that he claimed to have.

Medallion, 1990

The Medallion Corporation bought the 322 room Seelbach from Metropolitan Insurance for about $10 million. Medallion planned to build a two-story ballroom plus begin upgrades to the rooms.

Rap/Rock Singer, 1991

An angry young rap singer, who would go on to modeling and acting careers, started a fire outside his room, 942, after an altercation in 1991. The singer poured vodka on the carpet and set it on fire. He was charged by police with first-degree arson.

This was not one of the better moments for the hotel and the many entertainment groups that have stayed at the hotel.

The relationship between hotels and rock groups is always an uneasy one. Some groups would announce at the end of their concerts that there would be a party at the Seelbach Hotel. Some would move furniture into the hallway and others broke lights or set off fire extinguishers. But nothing was quite like the incident of 1991, which made the national news and required the rapper to return to Louisville later for a court appearance.

Expanding, 1994

Work started this year on the new ballrooms on the west side of the hotel. This area had been the rear motor lobby and a big part of the old Blue Boar Cafeteria.

The hotel's meeting space had a seating capacity for an additional 1,100 people when the expansion was completed in September, 1995.

The new ballrooms and meeting rooms had an outside entrance off of Muhammed Ali Boulevard, and were called the Medallian and Mezzanine Ballrooms.

General Manager Leaves, 1995

Michael Carnovale left the Seelbach after nearly ten years as general manager to pursue private business interests.

Mr. Carnovale, along with The Greater Louisville Convention Bureau, was primarily responsible for the rise in occupancy during his tenure.

David Nichols took over as general manager on April 1, 1995. He was the general manager at a Houston hotel owned by Medallion Hotels Inc.., which had owned the Seelbach for the past three years.

Fourth Avenue, 1995

Fourth Avenue and Muhammad Ali Boulevard, for the past 25 years the windiest corner in Louisville, returned to vibrancy and became alive and well in the mid-1990s because of the efforts of Mayor Jerry Abramson and the Downtown Development Corp.

Between the 1930s and 1960s the street had Louisville's best shopping, as well as the anchor of the Seelbach Hotel. Stewart Dry Goods across the street was Louisville's answer to Saks or Macy's in New York. Rodes, Selman's and other stores, theatres and restaurants adorned this area.

In the 1990s, after a 25-year period of downtown neglect and demise, the Seelbach Hotel came back after being closed from 1975 to 1982. The Starks Building, Rodes Clothiers, National City Bank and a coffee shop were also open and Fourth Avenue was alive again. All of this was a precursor to the arrival in 2004 of the ultimate booster to Louisville's famed corner, Fourth Street Live, a multimillion-dollar entertainment complex.

■ *Fourth Avenue, looking south in front of the hotel.*

All Wet, October 11, 1995

Russian Premier Mikhail Gorbachev came to town in 1995 to receive a Grawemeyer Award from the University of Louisville. As he arrived, Mr. Gorbachev's pants got soaked when he was caught in a sudden rainstorm at the airport.

Not having a change of clothes, the former Soviet leader gave his pants to one of the officers from the Louisville Police Dignitary Protection Unit. The police officer rushed the pants to a bellman at the Seelbach, who took them to be cleaned and pressed at a nearby cleaner.

While thousands of people waited at the Louisville Gardens for Gorbachev's speech, he was waiting for his pants.

The pants were returned to Mr. Gorbachev by the bellman a short time later.

Mr. Gorbachev arrived at The Gardens only 45 minutes late.

Gangsters, 1982 and 1996

John Young, the bellman at the hotel from 1982 to 1987, and Max Allen, a third generation barman, son of Max "Scopie" Allen, the bartender in the Rathskeller from 1918 to 1922, told this story to the author.

Al Capone, Dutch Schultz and Lucky Luciano visited the Seelbach during the Roaring '20s, perhaps prompted by hotel owner Abraham Liebling from Chicago, to do a little friendly gambling,

■ *(Above) Bartending legend Max Allen at the Seelbach Bar. (Right) Al Capone, a frequent Seelbach guest.*

which was, of course, illegal. The door to the Poker Room where they hung out was spring-loaded, and if the police happened to come into the lobby someone would push a button and the doors would close and the players knew to get their money off the table.

Stories have been told about Al Capone playing cards one night in the late 1920s when the door suddenly closed. He got up and went through a small hidden door to a staircase that went down to the basement kitchen, and from there he went down another staircase to the sub-basement and took the drainage tunnel under the city for several blocks.

The stairway leading from the poker room was put in as a way to get food to the billiard room from the kitchen.

■ *(Above) Troy Westrick seated in the old Poker Room with Al Capone's secret door behind him. (Below) The tunnel under the hotel.*

The Movie "The Insider," 1996

Director Michael Mann's "The Insider," the story of the man who blew the whistle on the tobacco industry, Louisvillian Jeffrey Wigand, starring Al Pacino and Russell Crowe, shot scenes at the Seelbach Hotel.

Several hotel associates were extras in the movie, including the front desk valet and the bell captain and his assistant. The lobby, 8th floor hallway and room 824 were the locations where the filming took place. The crew stayed at the hotel for about three months during the shooting of the film.

Sold Again, 1997

In 1997, Cap-Star purchased the Seelbach and five other hotels owned by Medallion Hotels. The announcement also said Cap-Star would buy three hotels in addition to those six, spending a total of $200 million.

$3.2 million was planned for upgrading the hotel. Cap-Star also said that Hilton would be managing the Seelbach.

The Ducks Are Coming

French master chef Jose Gutierrez is the widely-acclaimed chef at the Peabody Hotel, the historic Memphis, Tennessee hotel famed for its fine dining and the marching ducks that frolic in the hotel lobby fountain. The ducks have been a mainstay at the Peabody since the 1930s.

Chef Gutierrez and the Peabody Ducks are staying in the Presidential Suite for the weekend. There will be several times for everyone to bring cameras and view the only time the ducks will be appearing outside their own hotel.

The duck master from the Peabody will escort them from the ninth floor for their scheduled time in the Seelbach pond, which is set up in the center of the lobby.

Friday morning at 11:00 AM, there were about 100 people in the lobby and about 30 more on each side of the red carpet coming from the main elevators. The "Call to the Post" was sounded, the elevator door opened and, from the number of flashes popping from cameras, a person might have thought it was a Hollywood superstar stepping out to greet her public. Actually, it was better—the Peabody Ducks are here.

The ducks were escorted by the duck master from the Peabody and the honorary duck mistress, Ellen Minch, age nine, a fourth-grader at St. Matthews Elementary School.

Not to belabor the obvious, but the ducks, special as they are, are not potty-trained. The Presidential Suite was due for renovations soon after the ducks went back to Memphis.

The ducks are kept on the roof of the Peabody, in an indoor/outdoor enclosure. They stay at the hotel for about six months, and are then taken to a farm in Arkansas. After their wings grow back, it is their choice if they want to go live in the wild or stay on the farm.

The following week, a reporter stopped by and asked Mike Carnovale, the general manager, if the ducks were the messiest group

Office of the Mayor

Proclamation

To Whom All Those Present Shall Come, Greetings:

Whereas,   *it is a fowl day in the City of Louisville, Kentucky, and*

Whereas,   *some fine feathered friends from our neighboring city - Memphis, Tennessee- have winged their way to Louisville for a special visit; and*

Whereas,   *their visit to Louisville will undoubtedly goose the City's economy; and*

Whereas,   *people will flock to the Seelbach Hotel to get a gander at these very special guests; and*

Whereas,   *we would be daffy not to roll out the red carpet for this bevy of beautiful birds; and*

Whereas,   *all wise-quacking aside, there is just no ducking the fact that the City of Louisville fits the bill today as the Best Web Site in America.*

Now Therefore,   *I, Jerry E. Abramson, Mayor of Louisville, hereby proclaim January 16, 1998, as "Peabody Ducks Day" in the City of Louisville, Kentucky, and urge all citizens to recognize this special day.*

Peabody Ducks Day

Done in the City of Louisville, the Commonwealth of Kentucky, this Sixteenth day of January in the Year, the Nineteen Hundred and Ninety-eighth and of the City, the Two Hundred and Twentieth.

Jerry E. Abramson, Mayor

to have stayed in the Presidential Suite. His reply was, "No, that distinction goes to 'The New Kids on the Block.'"

The reporter asked what the difference was between the ducks and the "New Kids on the Block." His reply was, "The ducks can come back any time they want."

❧

President Bill Clinton, 1998

President Bill Clinton visited Louisville, and the Seelbach Hotel, in 1998. His visit included a public speech on health care at the Kentucky International Convention Center and a Democratic fundraiser at the Seelbach Hotel.

The Seelbach rolled out the red carpet for the President. It put a canvas roof up on Muhammed Ali Boulevard over the entrance and a red carpet on the ground. All associates were up to the task of helping with the security or keeping everything fresh and clean.

The day went without a hitch, and President Clinton left around 4:00 p.m.

❧

Fancy Feast, 1999

Since 1982, The Oakroom had always been a good restaurant. But in the late 1990s that changed. The Oakroom became a *great* place to eat, and in 1999 became a AAA Five Diamond Restaurant.

Many celebrities, politicians and sports figures have dined in the

Oakroom. The people that eat there rave about the food and the staff who take care of the preparation and serving.

Miss America Marries Lieutenant Governor, 2000

Miss America, Maysville, Kentucky's Heather French, was married in 2000 to Kentucky's Lieutenant Governor Steve Henry in a fairy tale wedding with about 1500 guests in attendance. The wedding took place at The Cathedral of the Assumption, a block from the hotel.

The hotel served as the staging area for the wedding. The bride was getting ready in the Fitzgerald Suite, with the help of her mother and family. The bell captain was asked to carry the wedding dress to the church. He went to the suite to pick up the dress and soon saw that he would need help. The dress and train was so big and beautiful it took six people to carry it across and down the street. Traffic had to be stopped.

Several hotel guests not with the wedding party said it reminded them of a movie or fairy tale. Everything was beautiful.

Sold Again, 2001

In 2001 Felcor Lodging Trust purchased the Seelbach Hotel and all the other properties of Meristar. The total of 113 hotels were acquired for $2.7 billion, in cash and stock.

The Seelbach continued to be managed by Meristar Hospitality Management Company, Meristar Hotels & Resorts, and a separate publicly traded company.

❧

Piano Man, 2001

April 27, 2001 was a day the Seelbach Hotel's associates and patrons of the Seelbach Bar will always remember.

The "Face to Face" tour of Elton John and Billy Joel was scheduled for Thursday April 28 at Freedom Hall. Billy Joel checked into the Seelbach on Wednesday, April 27. Later that night, he went into the Seelbach Bar to have a few drinks.

The band that was playing took a break around 9:00 p.m. Shortly thereafter, a gentleman walked up to the piano and started to play. No one paid much attention as it appeared to be just someone playing the piano.

The man playing the piano started to sing and then everyone realized it was Billy Joel. Before long the bar was packed. People were coming down from their rooms to hear him. Women were standing in the lobby in housecoats and curlers.

Billy Joel played and sang for about two hours. After he was finished, a writer from a local paper asked him why he played so long, and for free. His response was "No one made a request, took any pictures or tried to approach me."

His tour partner, Elton John, flew in the night of the tour and left immediately after it was over.

President Bush, 2002

President George W. Bush, in town to give a speech, invited Louisville's Little League World Series champions to tour Air Force One during his November trip to Louisville.

President Bush stayed at the Seelbach Hotel in room 930 for three hours before his speech at the Convention Center.

■ *President and Mrs. George W. Bush*

"Keep Your Distance," 2003

"Keep Your Distance," a drama/suspense film written and directed by Louisvillian Stu Pollard, shot many of its scenes at the Seelbach Hotel. The stars were Gil Bellows of "Ally McBeal" fame, Jennifer Westfeldt of the film "Kissing Jessica Stein", television veteran Stacy Keatch and Kim Raver. The shooting started on June 29, 2003.

Scenes of the front of the Seelbach Hotel and hallway on the Sixth floor, and shots around Louisville and Southern Indiana, are in the movie.

✤

Harriet Seelbach Jones, 2003

On January 8, 2003, Harriet Seelbach Jones died at age 84. Mrs. Jones' late husband, Warner L. Jones Jr., was a noted horseman and received the 1990 Eclipse Award of Merit for career contributions to horse racing. The ex-Chairman of Churchill Downs said he would not have been there if not for his wife.

Harriet Jones was the granddaughter of Louis Seelbach Sr. She was a graduate of Sarah Lawrence College, where she earned a degree in literature and art.

In 1939, she married Warner L. Jones. Harriet had never been around horses. Her husband owned a horse farm off U.S. 42 in Oldham County that would later become Hermitage Farm.

Thoroughbred horses and racing became her life. She put her

heart and soul into whatever she did. Hermitage Farm became one of the most recognized thoroughbred breeding farms in the country. In 1985, Warner Jones sold a yearling at the Keeneland sale for $13.1 million dollars. The price is still a world record.

Mr. Wilson Returns, 2004

Honeymoon nights are meant to create memories to cherish the rest of the happy couples' lives. During the early morning of April 25, 2004, at approximately 3:00 a.m., a just-married couple was sleeping on the eighth floor. The young man awoke from a deep sleep to feel cold air on his face. The room was extremely cold. He turned to look at his wife. She had the bedcovers up to her neck.

The young man looked toward the window and saw a figure of a man holding the drapes open as if he were looking out the window. Startled, the young man turned on the light by the bed. The room went back to its normal temperature and the figure by the window disappeared. The couple went to Hawaii the next day as planned. When they returned from their honeymoon they called the hotel concierge, an old friend, to let him know what had happened.

He told the couple and their family about the Lady in Blue, how she was seen in 1987 walking into the closed elevator doors on the 8th floor, around the corner from room 810, and also how she died in 1936. He told them that he thought Patricia Wilson had come looking for her husband in 1987, and he thought maybe in 2004 Mr. Wilson had come back looking for her. Hopefully, if this is so, they will both rest in peace now.

They asked what he thought about what had happened to them.

He explained that nothing ghostly had ever happened to him during his years of working at the Seelbach, but he thought they actually saw and felt something in their room on their wedding night.

Celebrities and Notables, 1905–1947

Stage performers: Nat Goodwin, Raymond Hitchcock, Della Fox, Mrs. Fiske and Fred Stone were among the many, as noted by Aulyn Kanston of Beverly Hills, California, in a 1949 column written to the editor of *The Louisville Times*.

Other famous people known to have stayed at the Seelbach during this time period were Charles Lindburgh and Lionel, John and Ethyl Barrymore.

Queen Wilhelmina and Princess Helena of The Netherlands visited the Seelbach and Jean Seelbach, Otto Jr.'s wife, was their escort while visiting such sites as "My Old Kentucky Home" in Bardstown, Kentucky.

Celebrities 1948–1975

Some of the celebrities who stayed in the Seelbach were recalled by Martha Smith, banquet manager at the time of the hotel's brief closing in 1975:

Eddie Cantor – singer and comedian

Joe E. Brown – comedian

Irene Dunn – Kentucky-born Hollywood actress

Faye Emerson – actress

Elvis Presley – the King of Rock and Roll

Minnie Pearl – comedian

Jackie Robinson – great baseball player

Jimmy Hoffa – union leader

Roy Rogers – actor (who refused all comps. He paid for everything he received.)

Liberace – entertainer (The hotel housekeeper took his sheets, tore them into little squares and sold them for $1 each).

Celebrities 1982–2004

After the hotel's re-opening in 1982, the celebrities kept on coming. The list includes: Whitney Houston, Carol Channing, Neil Diamond, Charlton Heston, James Earl Jones, Patrick Duffy, Randy Owens, Hank Williams, Jr., Miss Piggy, George Strait, Miss America Heather French, Dallas Cowboy Cheerleaders, Julia Child, Robin Williams, Mikhail Baryshnikov, Mikhail Gorbachev, Stacy Keach, Sinbad, Linda Gray, Eddie Albert, Jill St. John, the casts of *The Lion King* and *Phantom of the Opera*, Boy George, Al Pacino, Russell Crowe, N'Sync, Kevin Costner, Janet Jackson, Tony Bennett, Peter Jennings, Sarah Ferguson, Diane Sawyer, Vice-President Dick Cheney, Wolfgang Puck, and Rod Stewart and then-wife Rachel Hunter.

Singers

During the 1980s and 1990s, the Seelbach was a part-time home to a lot of singers.

Boy George, with all of his makeup, came to the hotel in the mid-1980s with his entourage. He was and still is the only entertainer to do things the right way. He checked in through the loading dock. His two buses were unloaded and all luggage and members of his staff were escorted through the service elevators. Not once during his stay did he ever go through the hotel lobby or out the front doors.

After delivering the luggage to everyone's room, I went to the Presidential Suite to see the road manager. While the road manager was arranging everything, I asked if Boy George would autograph a cassette cover. Before the manager could answer, this guy told me to bring the cassette to him and he would sign it. The next day I took the cover to his room. Boy George autographed it and sat and talked with me a few minutes about his music. Boy George was certainly a nice person, and not what I had expected.

Neil Diamond and his entourage occupied the entire ninth floor during their stay. The first morning of their stay, I was called to bring Cokes and ice to his room around 4:00 a.m. When I got off the elevator, a security guard stopped me and asked a few questions and then escorted me to room 924. When the door opened, it was like walking into a bar. Several band members had been playing cards all night and the smoke was thick from cigarettes.

Whitney Houston liked her privacy. She also entered the hotel through the rear motor lobby and left the same way. If she went out front, she would have on sunglasses, a baggy hat and regular clothes.

Randy Owens, the lead singer for Alabama, came to the hotel on several different occasions. The first time was for a concert and, being a country boy, he was easy to talk to and we got to know each other by first name after a few visits. Randy would come to all the cattle shows at the Fairgrounds and bring his sons with him. He would always go to the Fairgrounds early in the morning, usually before 6:00 a.m.

One morning, Randy and his sons came down a little earlier and there was a Delta airline crew waiting for the airport shuttle. Randy stopped to say hello and also give me tickets for their show. After he walked out, I noticed these two flight attendants staring at him, and they asked me who he was. I told them his name and they had a look on their faces, like who is that? After a few seconds, I said "Alabama." They ran to the front door, but he was gone.

You never know what to expect from celebrities, but always expect the unexpected.

Ladies of Television

Christmas came early for the Seelbach in 2003. *The Graduate*, starring Linda Gray as Mrs. Robinson, was playing at the theater in December.

Mrs. Gray wanted to know as much about the hotel as the city, as time would allow. She would stop and talk to the staff and was always smiling. Unlike many of the movie stars that have stayed at the hotel, she wanted to go to the restaurants where the locals ate and not the fancy ones. She is and was too nice for J.R. Ewing.

In November of 2005, Stephanie Powers of "Hart to Hart" came to town for *The King and I.* Janesha Russell, the sales representative for Ms. Powers, learned through her sources that the second day of Ms. Powers' visit was her birthday and that coconut cream cake was her favorite. Ms. Russell found Williams Bakery in Indiana, which made the cake, and she enlisted the help of Rob Goins to accompany her to pick it up. What a nice surprise for Ms. Powers. It seemed like all her friends sent her white lilies for her birthday, again her favorite.

On one occasion, the lobby concierge was delivering flowers and met Ms. Powers. She quickly told him to call her Stephanie. He told her a story about meeting her costar from "Hart to Hart," and how he had made a mistake and called Mr. Wagner's room and woke him up. He was so upset. She told the concierge that he deserved it.

These two ladies that graced the Seelbach are truly stars on and off the screen.

Sports Figures, 1982–2004

During the first 23 years of the second new beginning, sport figures from all sports have visited the Seelbach.

The most popular sportsmen were:

Boxing: Muhammad Ali, Rudy Ellis, and Mike Tyson.

The jockeys: Sandy Hawley, Canada; Frankie Dettori, England; Lester Piggott, England; and Eddie Delahoussaye.

Thoroughbred Trainers: D. Wayne Lucas (Thunder Gulch, Winning Colors and Grindstone) and John Sherriff (Bertrando).

Owners: Bob and Beverly Lewis (Silver Charm); Debi and Lee Lewis (Personal Hope); Barry Schwartz (Three Ring); and my favorite, Penny Chenery (Secretariat).

Baseball: Mark Grace, Cubs and Diamondbacks, as well as minor league teams.

Basketball: Rick Majerus, formerly of Utah; Roy Williams, Kansas and North Carolina; and Rick Pitino, UK, Boston Celtics and UofL.

Basketball Players: Nancy Lieberman of the WNBA and many other local players who made it to the pros.

Field Hockey: 2003 National Champions, Wake Forest.

Golf: Arnold Palmer, Vijay Singh, Davis Love III, Justin Leonard, Hideo Tanaka, John Daly, Colin Montgomery and Darren Clarke, just to name a few.

Tennis: Rod Laver and Martina Navratilova.

The Stones

There has never been as much excitement and commotion among people for any political figure or celebrity as there was the night of the Rolling Stones concert at Churchill Downs. About 500 people stood outside on the street, at the doors and in the lobby, to get a glimpse of these never-ending aged rockers from England. Jon McFarland, the general manager, and Jim Meyer, director of sales, had the job of escorting the group one-at-a-time to vehicles parked and waiting in front of the hotel.

The concierge's desk was inside the front doors entering the lobby. Nonie Fischer and Betty Johnson (Larry Johnson's 87-year-young mother-in-law and wife) were sitting waiting for Larry. Jon McFarland and Jim Meyer came off the elevators with the last Stone, Ron Wood. They stopped in front of the concierge desk and Nonie Fischer turned red as a rose. The deputy sheriff said, "We've got to go." Ron Wood yelled out, "Let's rock and roll." He did stop and give a few autographs and some picture time.

After the lobby cleared, I asked my mother-in-law if she was all right. Her response was, "Who was that old fart? He winked at me." I told her to ask her grandsons who Ron Wood is.

We thought the Stones were a demanding group. Their paperwork listed special water, couches, TVs, etc. This information was sent by the road manager, and when Mick Jagger, Keith Richards, Ron Wood and the others arrived at their rooms, they were surprised with all the extras.

The Kentucky Derby

Years ago, there was a track announcer by the name of Freddy Capossela. He would announce about one minute to post, "As the crowd is getting closer to the track, and the horses have reached the starting gate, that could only mean one thing . . . it is now post time."

The most exciting two minutes in sports comes to Louisville once a year.

The owners, trainers, celebrities and people from all parts of the world gather to see the first leg of the Triple Crown. All the hopes cling to what might be a Triple Crown winner, another super horse in the making. The Seelbach Hotel is a popular place for the visitors during that first weekend in May.

Trainer D. Wayne Lucas was a frequent visitor who stayed at the hotel during the spring meet at Churchill Downs. He saddled Winning Colors in 1988. In 1993, the hotel started getting more owners than in past years. Here are a few:

1993	Debi and Lee Lewis	Personal Hope, finished fourth
1995	Beverly and Robert Lewis	Serena's Song and Timber Country
1997	Beverly and Robert Lewis	Silver Charm, Won the Derby
1999	Beverly and Robert Lewis	Charismatic, Won the Derby

Penny Chenery, the owner of Riva Ridge, winner of the 1972 Kentucky Derby and Big Red (Secretariat), the winner of the Triple Crown in 1973, stayed at the Seelbach in 1998 for the 25th anniversary of Secretariat, and a few times in early 2000. She had to syndicate Secretariat in order to raise enough money to settle the tax department on her father's estate. He died January 3, 1973, before Secretariat won the Kentucky Derby.

With the change of the century in 2000, Beverly and Robert Lewis had two horses in the Derby. It was beginning to look like we could not run the Derby without the royal couple of horse racing. All of the Dogwood Stables owners, trainers, etc. stayed to see if Trippi could win.

February of 2006 brought a sad cloud over the horse racing industry. We lost two of the fine gentlemen of racing on the same day. Robert Lewis and Mr. Chapman, owner of Smarty Jones, passed on.

For the 2008 Derby, the Seelbach had a rare happening. The

owners of the first, second and third place finishers stayed at the hotel. What should have been a most exciting night, ended up being a sad affair, when the filly, Eight Bells, who ran second in the Derby, fell in the first turn after the finish and broke her two front legs.

The 2011 Kentucky Derby winner was Animal Kingdom. His owners are Barry Irwin and Carl Pascarella. Mr. Pascarella stays at the Seelbach every Derby. I guess we can say the Seelbach is a place where "winners stay."

The New Seelbach "2009"

The Monday after the 2007 Kentucky Derby, changes were about to happen for the Seelbach. Investcorp International, Inc. was putting 14 million dollars into a complete renovation of the hotel, inside and out.

Masonry work was to be done as well as windows, chandeliers and the ballroom. All rooms were re-done and new furniture added. The lobby became a new vital spot in the hotel with the addition of re-set lighting, remodeled skylight with its own special lighting system. This makes the lobby brighter for all guests to see.

The building became a "new" old beautiful hotel inside and out in 18 months. The work started in May, 2007, and was completed in January, 2009.

■ *The Seelbach lobby during construction (above) and completed (below).*

July 20, 2010: Seelbach Family Tour

Part of the Seelbach family visited the hotel to try to re-live some of their family history and pass on the story, as they were told, how Louis Seelbach II, the founder of the hotel, settled in Louisville.

This is just a small portion of the family tree to let you know who is who.

Louis Seelbach II had three children: Louis III, William Otto and Mary Helen. Louis III had four children: Harriet Blanch, who married Warner L. Jones; Helen Louise, who married Louis Rogers Hardy; Albert Peck, who married Pauline Huber; and Louis IV.

Members of the Helen Louise Hardy and Albert Peck Seelbach families visited to take a tour of the hotel that their great-great grandfather had built in 1903–1908.

Pauline Huber, Albert Peck's second wife, told how Louis II ended up living in Louisville. The Seelbach family moved from Germany in the mid-1860s and settled in Cincinnati, Ohio. There was a large population of German immigrants living in that area at that time.

In 1869, Louis decided to move south to Louisville, Kentucky, because it was a small town with more opportunities.

Ms. Huber told me the family moved from Germany because of the Prussian War and because they were afraid the sons would be drafted. In her words, in a roundabout way, the brothers were draft dodgers.

Family members in attendance:

Pauline Huber
Doug (Pauline's son) and Beth Seelbach

■ *The Seelbach family tour, left to right: Craig and Debi Hardy, Beth Seelbach, Pauline Huber, Doug Seelbach, and Rog Hardy*

Craig (Helen Louise's son) and Debi Hardy
Rog Hardy (Helen Louise's son)

The name Louis Seelbach lives on as Louis V and Louis VI live in Tucson, Arizona.

A special thanks to Bill Seelbach, who was not present for the tour, for putting it together and supplying me with the family tree and picture.

I can truly say meeting Louis Seelbach's family was a highlight of my 29 years with the hotel.

Presidents

In its first 70 years from 1905 to 1975 the Seelbach had more Presidents visiting than in the last 23 years. The following Presidents stayed overnight at the Seelbach:

William Howard Taft	1911
Woodrow Wilson	1916
Warren G. Harding	1922
Franklin Roosevelt	1938
Harry Truman	1948
John F. Kennedy	1962
Lyndon Johnson	1964
Jimmy Carter	1976

■ *John F. Kennedy and Lyndon Johnson*

William Howard Taft

Jimmy Carter

Woodrow Wilson

Harry Truman

❧

Seelbach Cookies

9 ½ ounces butter
7 ounces granulated sugar
5 ounces brown sugar (light)
3 eggs
1 tsp. vanilla
½ tsp. lemon juice
1 tsp. baking soda
½ tsp. cinnamon
1 ½ ounces oatmeal (dry)
7 ½ ounces cake flour
7 ½ ounces high gluten (bread flour)
16 ounces chocolate chips
12 ounces pecans

Cream butter and both sugars together with a paddle, add eggs one at a time. Add vanilla and lemon. Mix all dry ingredients and incorporate into sugar mixture. Add chocolate chips and pecans, mix just long enough to incorporate evenly. Bake at 350° until outside layer is slightly firm and inside is soft.

Makes approximately two dozen.

Seelbach Cocktail

Folklore or truth, the Seelbach Cocktail was made by accident in 1917 in the Seelbach Bar. The bartender opened a bottle of champagne which began to foam over, so he held it over two Manhattans that were sitting on the counter and the house drink was born.

How to make a great Seelbach Cocktail:

5 ounces champagne
1 ounce good Kentucky bourbon
Orange liqueur and bitters
Add a dash of sophistication
Serve it in a champagne flute with a twist of orange peel

All photographs in this book are courtesy of the Seelbach Hilton Hotel and Jon McFarland, except for the following: